T0177072

THE HUNCHBACK OF SEVILLE

BY
CHARISE CASTRO SMITH

★

★

DRAMATISTS
PLAY SERVICE
INC.

THE HUNCHBACK OF SEVILLE was originally produced in June 2014 by Washington Ensemble Theatre. It was directed by Jen Wineman, the scenic designers were Antoinette Bianco and Cameron Irwin, the costume designer was Desiree Jones, the sound designer was James Schreck, the lighting designer was Marnie Cummings, the props designer was David Rodriguez-Jenkins, and the stage manager was Joceline Wynn. The cast was as follows:

MAXIMA TERRIBLÉ SEGUNDA .... Samie Detzer
HRH QUEEN ISABELLA .... Maria Knox
INFANTA JUANA .... Libby Barnard
ESPANTA .... Rose Cano
TALIB FUROZH .... Ali el-Gasseir
ABDUL HASEEB .... Benito Vasquez
MAID .... Leah Salcido Pfenning
CHISTOPHER COLUMBUS/
DEPUTY GOVERNOR OF HISPANOLA .... Devin Bannon

THE HUNCHBACK OF SEVILLE was developed at the Brown/ Trinity Playwrights Repertory Theatre 2013 season under the artistic direction of Kenneth Prestininzi. It was directed by Taibi Magar.

CHARACTERS

CHRISTOPHER COLUMBUS
Christopher Columbus

ONE
a native of the Americas whose name was lost to history

TWO
a native of the Americas whose name was lost to history

ESPANTA
an old serving woman

MAID
*a wretched, timid little creature serving as a maid in the
house of Maxima Terriblé Segunda*

MAXIMA TERRIBLÉ SEGUNDA
*twin sister of Queen Isabella; aunt of Infanta Juana;
second in line to the Spanish Throne; a master cartographer;
the Hunchback of Seville*

ABDUL HASEEB
an old serving man; a Moor

INFANTA JUANA
*twenty-four-year-old princess of Spain;
daughter of HRH Queen Isabella;
will go on to become Queen Juana the Mad*

TALIB FUROZH
Maxima Terriblé Segunda's algebra tutor and lover; a Moor

HRH QUEEN ISABELLA
of Spain

DEPUTY GOVERNOR OF HISPANIOLA
the Deputy Governor of Hispaniola

TIME AND PLACE

The year is 1504.

- Which was twelve years after Christopher Columbus' fateful voyage to the landmass now known as North America. And also the last year of Queen Isabella's life.

All the action of the play (except the prologue) takes place over the course of twenty-four freakishly cold November hours in Seville.

- The average November temperature in Seville is 68° Fahrenheit.

All the action in the play takes place in the opulent bedchamber of Maxima Terriblé Segunda.

- The back wall is a gigantic map of the known world in 1504. With all the territorial divisions and names from back then. Small, handwritten notes are scribbled all over this map. Plastered all over the rest of the walls are other, smaller maps detailing specific regions of the world. There are towering, dusty stacks of books all over the room as well.
- The stage right wall has a large wooden door that leads to a hallway.
- The stage left wall has a large wooden door that leads to Maxima Terriblé Segunda's personal toilette. This contains a marble bath, which we can see.
- In the center of the room is a large mahogany four-poster canopy bed with many luxurious linens. Above her bed is an elaborate mobile of stars.
- Stage right there is a large mirrored armoire. Stage left there is a large table covered with many maps, a silken divan, and a trapdoor.

Take up the White Man's burden—
Send forth the best ye breed—
Go send your sons to exile
To serve your captives' need.
To wait in heavy harness
On fluttered folk and wild—
Your new-caught, sullen peoples,
Half devil and half child.

—Rudyard Kipling, 1899

"God then called me to run for the United States Congress. And I thought, What in the world would that be for? And my husband said, 'You need to do this.' And I wasn't so sure. And we took three days, and we fasted and we prayed. And we said 'Lord, is this what You want? Is this Your will?' And after—along about the afternoon of day two—He made that calling sure. Who in their right mind would spend two years to run for a job that lasts for two years? You'd have to be absolutely a fool to do that. You are now looking at a fool for Christ. This is a fool for Christ."

—Michele Bachmann, 2006

"If this is going to be a Christian nation that doesn't help the poor, either we've got to pretend that Jesus was just as selfish as we are, or we've got to acknowledge that he commanded us to love the poor and serve the needy without condition—and then admit that we just don't want to do it."

—Stephen Colbert, 2011

THE HUNCHBACK OF SEVILLE

Prologue: The New Effing World

*October 12, 1492. 3 A.M. Christopher Columbus lands on
the shore of the Bahamas, Spanish flag in hand. Christopher
Columbus speaks in an affected European manner.*

CHRISTOPHER COLUMBUS. My name is Christopher Co-
lumbus
And I claim this whole entire land-place that you all people see here
before you and which we can legally term
"The West Indies"
Since we obviously did our goal and got to India
In the name of Spain and all its subsequent domicilios, provinces
and corporations.
> *The crew kind of cheers. Christopher Columbus does a Zack
> Morris "time out."*

These are the true feelings I carried within my heart-breast on this
most momentous moment in world universal history:
My name is Cristoforo Colombo and I claim this whole entire
land-place
THE NEW FUCKING WORLD
In the name of me me me Cristoforo Colombo!!
And I hereby wish my máma was here to see this because she would
be really proud of me and also let it hereby be known that although
the repercussions and enormity of this discovery are yet unbe-
knownst to my conscious mind, deep in the eaves of my brain I
know, oh bambino do I ever know that I have found something
here on these virginish shores which will prove even more alluring

than, indeed, all the perfumes and spices of Araby.

And to every small person in Genoa who looked at me and said: 'Ooooh! Cristoforo Colombo is a poopy little kid who works at his daddy's cheese stand and is largely self-educated and misinterpreted much of what he read as modern historians have pointed out from the notes he made in the margins of his copy of *The Travels of Marco Polo* and also he poops his pants!"

And to everybody back in Europe who dares to think in private or utter in public: "I think privately and say publicly that there is a compelling body of evidence that Christopher Columbus did not actually reach India like he said he did because according to widely accepted calculations of how big the actual Earth is, there is no way that a boat during our times could go so fast that it would reach India without them running out of provisions and starving to death…"

And to everybody in the modern days who's like:

"You are a backwards imperialist douchebag with an overinflated ego and also you are responsible largely for one of history's most horrible genocides"

I say:

"Do YOU have a holiday named after you in the United States of America 505 years after your death?"

Okay, so guess who is famous and guess who is not.

> *Zack Morris "time in." The Spaniards begin to play a patriotic tune on their drum and fife and do an elaborate ceremony where they stick the flag in the ground, bless the flag, talk about how awesome they are for getting to India. This goes on in pantomime as the next bit of dialogue happens.*

> *Two Native People appear in the shadows with weapons. They whisper. Supertitles are projected somewhere onstage.*

ONE. Our language is largely lost to history.

TWO. Largely, it is.

And so we will make use of translators and have people pretend we are speaking our native language.

ONE. Also, our names are lost to history and so alas

Even politically liberal playwrights in *(Year of performance.)*

Have no idea what would even be appropriate names for us to have…

TWO. Or what to wear.

ONE. This is sadly true.
We shall thusly be named by number only.
I am One.
TWO. And I am thusly Two.

A moment of sadness.

Hey One,
Do you think we should ambush those people in the big boats?
Because clearly if we wanted to we could, you know,
Use our extensive knowledge of these islands to ambush and kill them.
ONE. Yeah Two, we probably could.
Actually it makes sense that we most definitely could.
Just as the actual people who spied on Columbus and his men from the mangrove trees when they first landed in the Bahamas that fateful moonlight night could definitely have chosen to do.
TWO. Yeah they could have.
But based on the fact that Christopher Columbus lived to tell the tale of October 13, 1492, they did not make that choice.

They ponder this for a moment.

So hey let's not be jerks.
Let's try using…
Diplomacy.
'Cause probably like if we treat them with respect they'll do the same to us, right?
ONE. Probably…

> *They lower their weapons and disappear into the shadows.
> The volume gets turned up on the Spaniards singing a rousing
> chorus of a song like "We Are the Champions"* in thick Spanish
> accents. Lights fade out.*

---

* See special note on songs and recordings on copyright page.

ACT ONE

Scene 1

It's 7 A.M. on a freakishly cold morning in Seville. We half-see the figure of a woman in a bathtub, in her personal toilette. She's balding; her scalp is sort of patchy and scabby. She wears really thick glasses. She is Maxima Terriblé Segunda, the Hunchback of Seville. There are at least a couple of real live cats in the bathroom with her. She is reading The Compendious Book of Calculation by Completion and Balancing *to them in the original Persian. Suddenly, the servant Espanta bursts in the door of the bedchamber, out of breath.*

ESPANTA. That is what you *get* Maxima!!!!
That's what you get—
For ignoring not one
Or two or two and a half
But THREE
Summons from Her Royal Highness Queen Isabella of Spain.
We just received word that she's on her way.
She'll be here any moment now.

> *No response. Espanta shivers. To audience:*

Oh hello, I had not seen you there.
Hello gentle spectators.
Welcome to our play.
As you can see, there is a big problem underway.
An unplanned visit from the most powerful woman in the world,
At seven A.M. on the coldest morning Seville has ever seen.
Maxima Terriblé Segunda?
I know that you are in your personal toilette for I hear your splashes in the tub-basin.

> *From behind the great wooden door.*

MAXIMA. Go away, for I am not here.

ESPANTA. You are here!
For your speaking confirms it.
MAXIMA. It's too cold.
ESPANTA. I grant you that today it is freakishly cold for November in Seville but that does not supersede the fact that Her Royal Highness Queen Isabella of Spain and her daughter Infanta Juana, Princess of Spain, will be here in mere minutes and it is not fit you should receive them from your commode.

> *Espanta flies around tidying up the room. A Maid enters, timidly, with a feather duster. The Maid's back is slightly hunched; she walks with a bit of a limp. The Maid stares at the room and its maps, slack-jawed and slightly mystified.*

Hey you!
Gawk less and dust harder.
MAID. Of course, Your Ladyship.
ESPANTA. *(Points to the bathroom.)* In *there's* the lady.
This ancient pile of bone is Espanta and that's that.
And you are?
MAID. New! My name is Innocenzia. Today is my first day...
Lady... Espanta... Ma'm...
ESPANTA. Well Innocenzia, you'll be out on your heels before the sun sets if you don't help me get this heap looking presentable.
Presently.

> *The Maid starts dusting the maps, slows down and stares at them. Espanta notices this and glares at her.*

MAID. Forgive me Espanta ma'm but I've just never seen such strange drawings before in my life. They're... beautiful.
ESPANTA. They're the pustous runoff of an overdeveloped feminine mind.

> *To the audience:*

Let this demented scrawling be a cautionary tale to young ladies everywhere about the dangers of excessive education.
MAXIMA. They're maps, you sordid troll. They're called maps.
ESPANTA. Go bang on the door again my girl.
Bang hard.

> *The Maid goes to the door and knocks politely.*

MAID. Ahm... excuse me for disturbing you in your personal toilette madam but well you see it seems that um well the Queen—

ESPANTA. COME OUT OF THE BATHROOM RIGHT NOW OR I'LL BREAK IN THIS DOOR I SWEAR TO JESUS!!

Nothing. The sounds of water splashing.

Go fetch me a crowbar dear girl.

The Maid exits in search of a crowbar. To audience—

Ah gentles,
I must admit that I am very relieved that you have come here today,
For finally I have some people in which to confide.
What's that you say?
You want to know about my life?
Pah… But I'm just an old serving woman!
Well, if you insist.
My post here has been… lonely and harsh.
For example, it has been challenging
Spending the last thirty-two years in this white-collar sort-of prison sort-of exile tower.
And, no. To answer your questioning mind,
It has not been easy simultaneously guarding and nurturing
The adopted royal genius freak in that bathtub in there since the day she was born—
I mean FOUND.
Not born that's not what happened,
(Directed at the bathroom.) I meant FOUND!
MAXIMA. Whatever…
ESPANTA. *(To the audience.)* I, who FOUND,
Fifty-two long years ago,
That hunchbacked spine and those crippled little legs
In a fateful bulrush basket
Outside the palace gates
On the same day
That is the birthday
Of the Queen.
Who is her adopted sister.

To Maxima:

Maxima mi amor, ya. Bath time se acabó.
MAXIMA. The cold gives me the creeps.
ESPANTA. Oh Maxima,
Surely a woman of your immoderate learning does not put credence

in the colloquial peasant prophesies about cold in Seville?
Ancient axioms such as:

Ominously:

"A cold day in Spain will end in some pain."
Or
"Brisk is the day when Seville has to pay."
Or
"Revenge is a dish best served cold. In Seville."
MAXIMA. Espanta,
If you'd ever bothered to read one sentence in your life you'd know
that temperature is completely unrelated to fate.
ESPANTA. What's that other one? It's on the tip of my tongue.
My mother used to say it all the time…
Oh yes!

Super ominously:

"A frost on Seville: Surely blood will be spilled."

To audience:

No worries though gentles.
I'm sure that probably won't happen in this play.

Super secret to audience.

But I'm a little scared that it might!!
MAXIMA. Espanta, please just go the heck away and let me take
a freaking bath in peace with my cats around me.
My freaking adopted sister Her Royal Highness Queen Isabella of
Spain can suck it.
ESPANTA. A most unbeseeming outburst!!!

To the audience:

But with goodly reason, bless goodly Jesus.
Her Royal Highness Queen Isabella and my Lady Maxima Terriblé
Segunda
Have been on rocky terrain ever since they were unrelated babies
Who shared the exact same birthday…

Espanta has a sudden great pain in her chest.

Damn you heart-breast,
Which prevents me from telling lies to the gentles!

She invites the audience in for a great confidence.

Please do not tell anybody this thing, gentle spectators.
But the story of me finding Maxima Terriblé Segunda in a bulrush basket is a false lie!
A most heavy and burdensome lie that I have carried within my heart-breast for lo these fifty-two long long years!
The true story behind this false lie is a large secret
That may well become a large plot point later in this play.

> *A big knock on the door.*

ZOUNDS!!!! What is to ensue??

Scene 2

> *The Maid enters, flustered.*

MAID. Señora! Señora you have un visitor—
ESPANTA. The Queen!?!
MAXIMA. Tell them que no estoy here.
MAID. A man. A man who is a,

> *She whispers:*

A Moor.
ESPANTA. Scandal and alarum!
MAID. But such a Moor-man as I have never seen before…
His face was hidden from me,
But he was cloaked in noble robes, and wore his hat at such a be-witching and rakish angle.
And Señora—
He asks that I should give you this.

> *The Maid produces a coconut on a velvet pillow. Espanta gasps—*

ESPANTA. What on the flat surface of God's great earth is THAT?
Some sort of heathenish shrunken head?
Dispose of it at once, maid.
MAXIMA. Do not dispose of it maid!
I shall emerge to collect it.

> *Splashing from within the toilette. The oaken door opens with*

16

a groan. Maxima Terriblé Segunda emerges wrapped in a towel. She has a painfully hunched back and crippled legs.

ESPANTA. Maxima Terriblé Segunda!
Clothe yourself at once or you shall catch your death of the rheum.
MAXIMA. Show me the favour, maid.

The Maid produces the coconut.

Wondrous…
Surely it must be the preservèd head of some noble New World beast.

She shakes the coconut and you can hear the milk sloshing around.

Listen!
For you can hear its brain humours sloshing around.
ESPANTA. Fetch me a basin maid, I shall be sick.
MAXIMA. Maid. Espanta. Leave me at once.
And maid, admit the gentleman in question to my chambré.
ESPANTA. Sirrah! But you are nude—
MAXIMA. Nude or clothed I remain your boss.
Maid, do as I say.
MAID. Yes Your Ladyship.

The Maid bobs and goes.

ESPANTA. Surely you do not think it to be
The Moor Talib Furozh—
MAXIMA. Well, he was wearing his hat at a bewitching and rakish angle—
ESPANTA. Your former tutor of algebra and secret lover—
MAXIMA. You heard the girl Espanta—
ESPANTA. The very Moor lover tutor that the Queen herself banished to the New World three years ago because she feared he was making you too smart for your own good?
MAXIMA. Who can say if it is he Espanta?
Who can rightly say?
But whoever this stranger may be, I take this most rare and precious gift as evidence of his goodly and charitable nature.
Go Espanta, do my bidding.

As Espanta leaves:

ESPANTA. Oh that I might use my brute strength to knock some decency and sense into that thick and misshapen skull!

Scene 3

Maxima Terriblé Segunda dresses herself as she speaks.

MAXIMA. Ah me, can it really be true?
Talib Furozh
Returned from the New World at so very long last?
My maid Espanta thinks she's the only one who can talk to the audience
But uhm, duh,
Not true.
Taliiiiib Furoooozh.
Whose name on my tongue feels as soft as a ruddy cheek.
As you can all clearly see,
I'm not a beautiful woman and I never have been,
I'm grotesque and frequently in pain
Like a tarred bird stuck in a jar.
Feared, loathed and mostly alone.
I mean, basically in this time period,
Which is Spain in 1504
People think that when a hunchback baby is born
It means that the parents were up to some wickedness.
Like, sexually.
And this being a Catholic country and all, the stakes on that can get a little high so...
It's a fairly common practice around these parts for hunchback babies to be
Abandoned in baskets or buckets on doorsteps.
I know this because that's exactly what happened to me.
Espanta found me in a basket outside the palace gates fifty-two years ago.
And the royal family was all
"Awww since we're so nice and good Catholics and everything we will take in this little hunchback bastard to show everybody how nice we are!"
So blah blah blah

Isabella and I were raised together,
Yada yada I turned out to be way smarter than Isabella
Next thing you know Isabella becomes Queen and I'm relocated to
this tower unloved and alone with my books until...
He
Was allowed to come here and teach me algebra to keep me enter-
tained. And then
He
Tamed me and taught me to sail my own raging waters.
He
Put a compass in my palm and said:

> *Magically appears:*

TALIB FUROZH. "North is always north.
The stars move like so.
Numbers are mysterious but ultimately knowable.
Y=mx+b."

> *Magically disappears.*

MAXIMA. This map of the wide world,
Plotted with numbers and by stars,
Is the map too
Of our love!
What an improbable set of coincidences have coincided
Resulting in my adopted sister the Queen whom I hate
To be coming here the same day as my great love Talib Furozh
whom I love.

> *She has put herself together quite magnificently over the course
> of her speech. There is a knock at the door. Maxima Terriblé
> Segunda strikes a sexy pose on her bed.*

You may approach—

Scene 4

A rakishly-hatted, cloaked man whose face we cannot make out enters the room.

ABDUL HASEEB. My lady!

MAXIMA. Talib my love!

> *She runs to him, tears off his cloak and tries to start making out with him. It is Abdul Haseeb, the old-man confidante of Talib Furozh.*

Abdul Haseeb!

Gross.

> *She backhands him.*

I thought you were Talib Furozh, my true lover!!

ABDUL HASEEB. I beg your pardon my great lady.

I borrowed these clothes from my master,

Correctly believing I would be mistaken for him

And that I would thusly gain access to your person.

Talib Furozh is—

MAXIMA. Tell me immediately—

Does Talib Furozh live?

ABDUL HASEEB. He lives!

But 'twere better methinks that he had perished.

> *She slaps him again.*

MAXIMA. Do not utter such a sentence about Talib Furozh.

ABDUL HASEEB. Oh lady, to have lived to see what these old exhausted eyes have seen.

I've a letter milady.

Penned to you by Talib Furozh himself right before he attempted to—

MAXIMA. Give it to me right now!

Gimme it!!

> *Abdul Haseeb hands her the letter.*

Scene 5

In a separate light, Talib Furozh appears and narrates his letter to Maxima Terriblé Segunda. Sounds of musket fire, screams, ocean waves, and Arabic music underscore his narration.

TALIB FUROZH. A final favor to the fairest lady ever I laid eyes on,
My benefactress and pupil,
My true lover and friend, Maxima Terriblé Segunda.
Dated the 23rd day of October,
1504 A.D.
MAXIMA. His very hand!
Dated one month ago, Abdul Haseeb.
TALIB FUROZH. Maxima,
By the time you get this letter I'll be gone.
MAXIMA. Gone where?
ABDUL HASEEB. Oh milady…
TALIB FUROZH. As you know, three years ago I left from the port of Cádiz,
Guided by the map we so lovingly drew as one.
We reached Hispaniola in four short weeks.
Attempting to make the best of our banishment and eager to explore a land we'd only dreamed of,
Abdul Haseeb and I rowed a small boat to a beach, which to our visage lay beneath a thick covering of white seashells…
Our horror and trepidation grew to a feverish pitch as we approached to find the "seashells" were in fact a great blanket of human skeletons picked clean and bleaching in the sun.
MAXIMA. O horrible!
Was it vicious serpents? Croc o' diles? Fearsome tygers?
TALIB FUROZH. No, milady.
For surely serpents and tygers are of a more genteel and feeling nature than the beasts responsible for this atrocity—
MAXIMA. What beasts?
TALIB FUROZH. Your very countrymen milady…
Have wrought upon the native populous of Hispaniola the most

21

pitiless and swift destruction that history has yet witnessed.

    Pause.

Lighting upon the beach, we found the surrounding native city burned to the ground and its former inhabitants all murdered or enslaved.
The piggish Spanish governor's bloody lust for gold knows no bounds.
Every Taíno man, woman, and child who is unable to fill a bell with gold is to be maimed.
I came to befriend an Arawak chief, Behechio, who told me that the inhabitants of the island had once numbered over three million.
Maxima, there were less than fifty thousand of them left.
He told me of babes ripped from the arms of their mothers, women raped, men literally roasted and laughed at. Tossed over cliffs and spit upon as they descended.
This really happened in history and I promise you I'm not making this up…
And so Maxima, farewell.
This simple mathematician's mind can no longer endure the torrent of horrors which nightly flood his dreams…

    Talib Furozh disappears.

Scene 6

MAXIMA. Abdul Haseeb I cannot begin to comprehend this letter.
You say Talib Furozh lives?
ABDUL HASEEB. Yes, he lives.
But this tale of woe is not yet over.
Directly after he penned this letter to you milady,
Talib Furozh snapped.
The outrage that had urged him to end his own life
Flowed outwards like a great bilious wave,
And I could only watch as he flung a blazing torch
Into the living quarters of the Governor of Hispaniola.
MAXIMA. Oh my God…
ABDUL HASEEB. We ran, boarded a boat
And narrowly survived the passage back to Spain.
We docked yesterday to find this

Abdul Haseeb produces a wanted flier.

The Governor of Hispaniola has placed a bounty on each of our
heads of one thousand reales.
Talib Furozh's person lives milady,
But his faith in mankind is gone.
He only asks how it may be that his life should be lived out
In such hopeless and barbaric times.
We must watch him day and night so that he does not kill himself.
MAXIMA. You must bring him to me at once Abdul Haseeb.
ESPANTA!!

Scene 7

Espanta comes in immediately.

ESPANTA. I was listening at the door milady!
I heard everything.
MAXIMA. My true and good Espanta! Abdul Haseeb, take this
gold
And use what means of conveyance you must
To bring Talib Furozh to my chamber undetected.
Go now!
ABDUL HASEEB. I will!
Abdul Haseeb leaves.

Scene 8

MAXIMA. Espanta,
What nightmares my true love Talib Furozh has endured!
And you poor murdered millions of the New World,
Is Spain's new day born from your blood?
ESPANTA. So it would seem, milady. So it would seem.
MAXIMA. Oh Espanta, I thought the New World was supposed

to be verdant, and peaceful.
And New.
This is fucked.
Go try and stall the Queen for a second.
I gotta figure some shit out.
ESPANTA. You got it.

> *To audience:*

Methinks I begin to fear now the colloquialisms about the cold, gentles.
Me fears them!!

> *Espanta goes. After a moment we hear manic giggling outside the door.*

MAXIMA. Espanta is that you?
Espan—

End of Act One

ACT TWO

Scene 1

Infanta Juana bursts through the door, laughing her head off. She is a beautiful twenty-four-year-old woman but she talks in a baby voice like she's seven. She has a little doll in her hands that's dressed like a prince.

INFANTA JUANA. Auntie Maxima! Auntie Maxima!
Felipe and I are weawwy weawwy happy to see wou.
Right Felipe?
> *She makes the prince doll "talk."*

Wight!
Felipe told me the funniest joke ever on the way over here Auntie Maxima—
MAXIMA. Seriously Juana,
Didn't your mother ever teach you to knock?
INFANTA JUANA. Do you like my new fu(r)w cape Auntie M?
It's made out of baby leopard skins.
Mommy made me wear it today because it's
SOO COOLD.
You know what Felipe told me about the cold Auntie M?
> *Ominously.*

"A chill in Seville bodes ill for young ladies, cattle, oranges… and Hunchbacks."
Except it's probably not true about young ladies.
MAXIMA. …
…
…
Where's the Queen? I thought you were coming together.
INFANTA JUANA. We wew(r)e!
But she was taking for-e-ver long to walk so I ran ahead of her because I was so excited to see you can I play with your maps?

MAXIMA. No.
You should have waited for her Juana!

Infanta Juana looks like she's going to start crying.

INFANTA JUANA. But I just wanted to see you weawwy bad…
MAXIMA. And why are you talking like a baby?
You're twenty-four years old.
Stand up straight and talk normal.

Suddenly not like a baby but like a pissed off Queen:

INFANTA JUANA. How dare you tell me what to do or how to talk you fucking cripple bitch!!!
Stop talking to me like that or I will tell Mommy to cut off your allowance RIGHT NOW!
I can do that you know because I'm the princess of Spain and you're just like SOME LAME DUCK BASTARD MONARCH or whatever.
And I CAN play with your maps if I want to because technically everything in the kingdom of Spain belongs to me and my mom and dad and that includes your maps and also this ugly fucking thing over here—

Picks up the coconut and throws it on the ground.

WHATEVER IT IS!!

She suddenly eerily calms down and giggles like outside the door.

Now it is my royal decree that you play with me and Felipe!
Boop!
You're not playing.
MAXIMA. What shall we play, Your Majesty?
INFANTA JUANA. Get your maps and put them on the bed!

Infanta Juana hops onto the bed and starts jumping up and down. Maxima Terriblé Segunda hobbles painfully over to her table, collects her maps and spreads them out on her bed.

I don't feel like weading, will you read the names of the pwaces on the map fow me?
MAXIMA. The Netherlands.
INFANTA JUANA. That's exactly whe(r)we Felipe the handsomest prince in the universe is from!
Read another one.

MAXIMA. Castile.

INFANTA JUANA. That's where I get to be Qwueen of when Mommy dies!

Read another one.

MAXIMA. Hispaniola.

INFANTA JUANA. I don't know what that is that's boring.

Why do you have a mad face?

MAXIMA. Juana, has your mother ever spoken to you about Hispaniola?

Or the New World?

INFANTA JUANA. I know all about the New World!

My baby leopard cape is from the New World.

Mommy and Daddy got me a dancing dwarf from the New World. I named him Gargamel.

MAXIMA. Mmm-hmm.

And did Mommy tell you anything else about the New World?

INFANTA JUANA. Uhhmm…

It's my dominion?

Why do you have a mad face again?

Why aren't you playing?

MAXIMA. Oh Juana…

The Maid knocks on the door.

Scene 2

INFANTA JUANA. You may entew!

MAID. Princess, milady

Her Royal Highness has arrived.

Infanta Juana suddenly stops acting like a three-year-old.

INFANTA JUANA. Show her in please maid.

You may put away the maps now Maxima.

Infanta Juana hands her the Felipe doll.

And you may put away your doll as well Maxima in a safe hiding place where the Queen may not find it.

For you are a big girl now Maxima and you must no longer play with dolls not even dolls that are named after your husband.

MAXIMA. Of course, Your Highness.

> *Maxima Terriblé Segunda hides the Felipe doll under the trapdoor near the divan. There is the approaching sound of extensive fanfare coming down the hall. Infanta Juana and Maxima Terriblé Segunda drop to their knees. Maxima's bedroom door opens with a great burst of light—*

Scene 3

> *HRH Queen Isabella enters the room. She looks gravely ill and is leaning on a cane. Infanta Juana and Maxima Terrible Segunda remain bowing.*

MAXIMA TERRIBLÉ SEGUNDA and INFANTA JUANA. Your Royal Majesty!

> *The door closes. The light and fanfare die.*

HRH QUEEN ISABELLA. Help us.

> *Maxima Terriblé Segunda and Infanta Juana rush to her side and escort her to the divan. They prop her feet up. Infanta Juana is now acting totally like a sane person.*

INFANTA JUANA. My royal mother!
How deeply it grieves me to see you in such a delicate condition.
I trust God that my hourly prayers for your swift recovery will soon be answered.
It is unfit that you should be out o' doors on such a bitterly cold day in your poorly state and surely there is a draft in this room.
May I get you a blanket Mother?

> *HRH Queen Isabella nods. To Maxima Terriblé Segunda—*

Fetch the Queen a blanket.

> *Maxima Terriblé Segunda gets the Queen a blanket and places it over her. HRH Queen Isabella speaks, very feebly.*

HRH QUEEN ISABELLA. Daughter, leave us to our adopted sister awhile so that we may speak plainly to one another.

INFANTA JUANA. My sainted mother,
Surely anything you say to your lowly adopted sister I am also fit
to hear!
HRH QUEEN ISABELLA. Daughter, leave us.
INFANTA JUANA. Why don't you trust me Mom?
I'm a grown woman.
I'm old enough to know whatever it is you're going to say to her.
HRH QUEEN ISABELLA. Daughter…
INFANTA JUANA. I can seriously handle it!

> *HRH Queen Isabella opens the trapdoor with her cane and uncovers the Felipe doll.*

HRH QUEEN ISABELLA. This again?
INFANTA JUANA. It's hers, not mine.
MAXIMA. It is not mine Your Majesty.

> *Infanta Juana starts to devolve into her former trainwreck self.*

INFANTA JUANA. She's lying!
She's just a liar liar pantaloons on fire hunchback liar cripple and I
can't believe you would believe her over me your own daughter plus
remember when the court doctor told you that the doll was just a
way for me to relieve stress about the fact that I'm supposed to
govern a vast empire soon remember when he said that so don't get
mad about the doll because remember it's just only a way to relieve
stress and doesn't mean I'm crazy or anything…
HRH QUEEN ISABELLA. Stop being naughty Juana, go.

> *Infanta Juana goes apeshit and throws a crazy freak out temper tantrum as she exits.*

INFANTA JUANA. AaaaaahhhhhhGGGGG!!!!
It's not fairit'snotfairit'snotfairit'snotfairrrrrrrrrr!!!!!
MOM. MOM. MOM. MOM.
LOOK AT ME. MOM.
I'm going to go have some hot cocoa WITHOUT YOU TWO
because
I HATE PLAYING WITH YOU ANYWAYS.
Come on Felipe let's get out of here.

> *Infanta Juana leaves, slamming the door behind her.*

Scene 4

The two sisters are left alone in the room together.

MAXIMA. Isabella…
HRH QUEEN ISABELLA. Maxima.
MAXIMA. You look well.
HRH QUEEN ISABELLA. We are dying, as you well know.
MAXIMA. Well I had heard rumors but—
It pains me so to hear that…
HRH QUEEN ISABELLA. It obviously pains us more.
MAXIMA. Obviously.
HRH QUEEN ISABELLA. We trust you're being fed well?
You look it.
MAXIMA. My thanks, Your Highness.
HRH QUEEN ISABELLA. We trust your accommodations in the tower to be commodious?
MAXIMA. I am your grateful, humble servant My Liege—
HRH QUEEN ISABELLA. And the unlimited supply of world literature, which we have graciously agreed to fund for you, it provides you with sufficient mental stimuli?
MAXIMA. Yeah.
HRH QUEEN ISABELLA. This leaves us to wonder what hardship it was that might have prevented you from responding to our invitations to court.
Adopted sister,
Thrice we summoned you to our presence and thrice you never showed up…
MAXIMA. Oh my gosh, you summoned me?
I seriously had no idea.
I accidentally dropped my messenger pigeon in the toilet
And it's been dropping scrolls left and right.
Plus I've been really busy with like reading, and my cats so…
HRH QUEEN ISABELLA. Of course.
All perfectly valid reasons to drag a dying monarch out into the cold.
MAXIMA. Anyways…

HRH QUEEN ISABELLA. Do you know why we've come here today Maxima?
MAXIMA. To visit or something? Or to gloat?
Or to banish the only person who ever loved me to punish me for being smart?
HRH QUEEN ISABELLA. We presume you're referring to the heretic mathematician whom we forcibly separated from his post as your tutor because his continued presence in Spain was a threat to national security?
MAXIMA. His name is Talib Furozh.
HRH QUEEN ISABELLA. Please know that we acknowledge the sacrifices that you have made in service of Spain's greatness.
MAXIMA. Wait. Was that like, an apology or something?
I'm confused—

> *Beat.*

HRH QUEEN ISABELLA. We look back on our life Maxima,
At how we have strived as Queen to listen to the will of the highest…
MAXIMA. Mmm-hmmm.
HRH QUEEN ISABELLA. To be his humble servant and to
Lead our flock always in the image of the Lamb of God…
MAXIMA. Yeah, no you totally have—
HRH QUEEN ISABELLA. We fasted and we prayed and we opened wide our heart
And do you know what happened Maxima?
MAXIMA. You heard voices in your head telling you to do some particular thing…?
HRH QUEEN ISABELLA. That's right Maxima.
The Lord our God, maker of heaven and earth
Revealed himself
To us.
MAXIMA. Wow.
HRH QUEEN ISABELLA. Wow is right Maxima.
Wow indeed.
And you know what he told us Maxima?
MAXIMA. I seriously have no clue.
HRH QUEEN ISABELLA. He said:
GOD. *(Voiceover.)*
And ye shall go forth to the crippled hunchback bastard child
And ye shall raise her up to meet your greatness
And yea she will rule Spain though she be a crippled hunchback bastard

that someone found in a bulrush basket.
HRH QUEEN ISABELLA. That's precisely what the Lord God
spake to us.
What think you… sister?
Speak.
MAXIMA. What about Juana?
HRH QUEEN ISABELLA. As we are sure you have been able to
discern
From spending even thirty seconds with her,
Juana is an imbecile and unfit to reign.
Your intellect Maxima,
Is a rare and precious gift from God,
And one that might shine a light on Juana's path.
You would be her advisor Maxima,
All of her actions would be directed by you.
It is hardly an uncommon state of affairs to have an idiot rule in
name only while other, more powerful parties run the show.
So?
What say you?
MAXIMA. Um, no.
HRH QUEEN ISABELLA. Pardon?
MAXIMA. I said no.
HRH QUEEN ISABELLA. Really?
MAXIMA. Yeah.
HRH QUEEN ISABELLA. Why?
MAXIMA. It's like a big deal for me to even leave my bathroom,
I have like, no people skills
And there's no way that your whacked out little bundle of joy out
there would ever listen to me so, no.
HRH QUEEN ISABELLA. Whoa.
We were not expecting you to turn down our offer.
We struggle to come up with a plan B.

> *A knock on the door.*

You may enter…

> *A repentant Infanta Juana enters. She is eating what appears
> to be one of those turkey legs you buy at Ren fairs.*

INFANTA JUANA. Hey Mom. Hey Auntie M.
I just wanted to say,
Sorry for how I was acting before.

It was really immature.

So, sorry.

And Mom,

I just wanted to say

That you don't have to worry,

'Cause I'm seriously gonna do a super awesome job all on my own

Of Queening the more or less entire planet Earth.

HRH Queen Isabella sniffs something nasty.

HRH QUEEN ISABELLA. Juana, what is that you're eating?

INFANTA JUANA. Roasted peasant.

HRH QUEEN ISABELLA. Roasted *pheasant*. You mean roasted *pheasant*.

INFANTA JUANA. No, I mean roasted peasant.

HRH Queen Isabella clutches her heart.

HRH QUEEN ISABELLA. Fetch us a surgeon, with haste daughter.

INFANTA JUANA. You heard her, you dumb-ass bitch—go get her a doctor.

Maxima Terriblé Segunda very painfully hoists the dying Queen onto her back. She drags her out the door to the hallway. Infanta Juana blows a bubble of bubble gum, sends a text, and follows them. They all exit.

Scene 5

The moment they leave, Talib Furozh pops out of the trapdoor. However he appeared in Maxima's imagination, he now looks about twenty years older. He's still handsome but his beard is really overgrown and he looks shell-shocked. He's on high alert, checks to see if anyone is hiding anywhere, hears someone coming and hides in the armoire. Maxima Terriblé Segunda enters, with Espanta right on her tail.

ESPANTA. You said WHAT?!?

MAXIMA. I said no, okay so stop freaking out already.

33

ESPANTA. You said no to being the advisor to the Queen of Spain? But why?!?
MAXIMA. Hello, Spain is fucked, Espanta.
Ninety-nine percent of the people who live here are right-wing Christian fundamentalists who most certainly would not accept a female atheist as their leader,
And the other one percent are stuck-up douchebag nobility who would spit on me for being a hunchback.
The New World is a freaking horrific bloodbath.
Why exactly would I want to take the helm of that?
ESPANTA. Well, someone's got to, right?
Why not you?

> *To Audience:*

I admit that the burdensome secret of my heart-breast, gentles,
Is not unrelated to milady Maxima's
Relationship to the throne.
MAXIMA. ...
...
...
...
Where is Talib Furozh?
ESPANTA. We found him milady, brought him to the castle but...

> *There is a shifting sound from within the armoire.*

MAXIMA. Leave us Espanta.
Go see that the Queen is made comfortable.

> *Espanta goes.*

End of Act Two

ACT THREE

Scene 1

MAXIMA. Oh at last…

> *She readies herself, goes to the armoire, flings it open… and she sees no one.*

Talib? Talib Furozh?

> *She steps into the armoire, and finally after a little while she emerges, leading Talib Furozh by the hand.*

TALIB FUROZH. Yes.

Yes.

Yes. I am here.

Please don't push me, I'm right here.

Please don't touch my skin.

MAXIMA. Darling, Talib my love come here.

I'm sorry I'm so sorry.

> *She attempts to embrace him. He pushes her away.*

TALIB FUROZH. It's cool.

It's just, seeing you is a lot to take in you know.

MAXIMA. Okay, I'm sorry.

I just missed you so much.

TALIB FUROZH. Cool.

It's real good to see you too.

> *He lets her embrace him. She holds him and he melts down but then suddenly can't take it and he squirms away from her. As if painfully trying to erase her touch from his skin but he can't. He despairs.*

Maxima baby, I'm so tired that I just want to die.

It's like, we roll into the world as these happy fat little gods right?

And if we've got any sort of luck our mothers love us and teach us for years that the world is not such a bad place—sure there's stuff we're not supposed to touch 'cause we'll get burnt or something but mostly if we can keep our bodies safe then we'll be okay and

35

afterwards we might even get a toy and go to sleep and dream…
But then as you grow up your start to realize that
It's not just keeping your hands away from flames but that there are
people out there that want to kill you just because you are a Moor
and the Queen of Spain decides that you and all your people need
to leave right away.
Or because you were an entire civilization of people living separate
lives an ocean away from Spain and then one day a bunch of cock-
holes on boats literally descend upon you and not only infect
everyone with foreign diseases but also torture and kill everybody
and then also kill your soul by telling you that you deserve it because
God hates who you are.
And you can come back home and hide away and be temporarily iso-
lated from the completely random utter brutality of the world but…
MAXIMA. But they're wrong.
You are gentle and good and gifted…
TALIB FUROZH. No.
I was there Maxima.
None of that matters.
I saw what those people did,
And I can never not know it.
I give up.
I just can't believe that I was born at such a relentlessly shitty point
in history and there's nothing I can do about it.

> *He starts sobbing. She sings this to the tune of "Twinkle Twinkle
> Little Star" very tenderly—it's a ritual that they have.*

MAXIMA. Sine. Cosine. Cosine. Sine.
TALIB FUROZH. Cosine. Cosine.
TALIB FUROZH and MAXIMA. Minus sine. Sine.

> *They kiss and we see two people who are truly in love.*

MAXIMA. There must be a way out of this.
Talib my love, let's just pack up our maps and blow this joint.
We can go anywhere we want.
TALIB FUROZH. I'm sorry but where exactly on earth right now
do you think we could run away to that would be safe for a Moor
wanted by the Spanish Crown and a fairly conspicuous agoraphobic
Hunchback?
MAXIMA. I don't know… China or something.
TALIB FUROZH. Yeah 'cause it's so easy to get there from here.

MAXIMA. I don't know!

   A beat.

TALIB FUROZH. What was that thing Espanta was saying before about the Queen?

MAXIMA. Isabella asked me to be Juana's advisor.

I said no.

For several reasons.

Not the least of which being that saying yes would mean losing you…

TALIB FUROZH. But Maxima, what if it meant just the opposite?

MAXIMA. Um?

TALIB FUROZH. What if you say yes,

And you turn this bitch around from the inside?

Think about it.

There are a lot of people in this country

Who would be amenable to your way of seeing things.

Pretty much everybody who lives here is scared shitless about getting killed for not acting Catholic enough so I think you'd probably have some support among them if you loosened things up a little…

And if you issue a decree that I'm not a wanted man anymore, and you tell them they have to stop all that shit that's going on over there,

Then who gets to tell you no?

MAXIMA. Okay that all sounds great but there's one big problem with that which is…

TALIB FUROZH. …

MAXIMA. That I'm nothing.

I'm sorry but, look at me.

I know you love me but from

An outside perspective I am actually less than nothing.

If I say yes to being Juana's advisor,

What advice am I supposed to give her exactly?

Because, (A) who would listen to me?

And (B) who should listen to me?

I don't have any answers,

All I have are observations and opinions.

Which are different than answers.

And who says that maybe I don't just somehow

Make things worse than they already are?

I'm scared.

TALIB FUROZH. Okay, but isn't the alternative way scarier?
MAXIMA. Yeah.
TALIB FUROZH. I'll help you.
We'll rewrite the map of history… together.
MAXIMA. Come here…
I missed you Talib.
TALIB FUROZH. I missed you too.

> *They start to make love tenderly. Right in the middle of it there is a clambering at the trapdoor. They have about three seconds for Talib Furozh to hide under the covers before—*

Scene 2

> *Infanta Juana pops out of the trapdoor.*

INFANTA JUANA. Supwise!
I came back Auntie M.
MAXIMA. Juana what did I tell you about knocking?!?
It is not okay for you to be here right now.
You need to leave.
INFANTA JUANA. Okay yeah except that remember before when I told you that you really cannot tell me what to do because I am going to be the Queen really soon?
That really still applies to right now.
MAXIMA. What do you want Juana?
INFANTA JUANA. Why are you in bed right now?
MAXIMA. I'm resting.
INFANTA JUANA. It's the daytime.
MAXIMA. …
…
…
…
INFANTA JUANA. What did you and Mama talk about before?
MAXIMA. Nothing interesting Juana…
INFANTA JUANA. You know what Felipe told me Auntie M?

That there's a special word for when someone tells a lie to the Queen. It's like branches or forests or…

MAXIMA. Treason?

INFANTA JUANA. That's it!

And that is really bad so you better not treason me at all right now.

MAXIMA. Okay, we were talking about tax laws.

I could explain it to you but I bet you would think it was really boring.

INFANTA JUANA. O 'cause I thought you were talking about that God told Mama you get to be my boss when she dies because she totally doesn't understand me at all and thinks I'm crazy.

MAXIMA. You were eavesdropping?

INFANTA JUANA. Yeah.

But no worries because I think it would be really awesome if you were my sidekick.

I could get them to make you like a little mini crown

That was just like mine only much much smaller.

Also I'm like pretty sure I heard a dude in here…

Was that your boyfriend Auntie M?

The M to the O to the O to the R.

I wanna see him!

MAXIMA. There's no one here.

Juana, I'm going to give you a chance to prove that you're a rational human being and turn around and go right back out that trapdoor and not say another word about what you saw or heard…

INFANTA JUANA. Why would I do that Auntie M?

MAXIMA. Because Juana I honestly believe that somewhere in there you have a capacity for reason and Juana you and I might just have the chance to do some really important work together really soon.

Would you like that?

INFANTA JUANA. What you mean that thing about like ending the Inquisition?

MAXIMA. Well that's one of the big things.

INFANTA JUANA. NO WAY!

You are so crazy Auntie M.

MAXIMA. What? How do you even know what the Inquisition is?

INFANTA JUANA. It's when we bring boats to that place on your map and kill people until they give us money 'cause Jesus likes us more.

MAXIMA. But do you know what the word genocide means
Juana?
INFANTA JUANA. What that there are like some casualties on
the path
To doing what's best in the interest of Spain?
Yeah, I get that.
But it's just like, they're all the way over there and we seriously need
gold right now and so like I really feel that like the pros outweigh
the cons if there even are any cons.
MAXIMA. You obviously don't get it Juana.
INFANTA JUANA. I obviously do get it.
'Cause duh Auntie M, how else are we supposed to get gold?
Who's a better ruler?
Somebody who wants to protect a bunch of devil-people she doesn't
even know?
Or someone who is trying to get a shit ton of money for free to
make her country mad powerful?
Sounds to me like you're the one who needs an advisor Auntie M.
When I'm Queen we're gonna think even bigger, cover more terri-
tory that's how come I wanted to see your maps before.
We need to start thinking big.
Like a lot a lot more gold.
And don't think I forgot about your boyfriend!
He(ll)woooo!!
Auntie M's maaannfriendddd??
Auntie M and Manfriend sitting in a t(r)wee
K-I-S-S-I-N—

> *Maxima creeps up behind Infanta Juana and clocks her on
> the side of the head with the coconut.*

G.

> *She goes down.*

Scene 3

MAXIMA. Oh no, Oh no, Oh no, Oh no, Oh no I killed her.
TALIB FUROZH. She's still breathing.

How long do you think your sister has left, Maxima?

MAXIMA. I don't know, from the looks of it maybe a couple of days.

A week tops—

TALIB FUROZH. So here's what I'm thinking.

We gag this bitch up and stick her in your bathroom.

I'll guard her in case she wakes up and you tell your sister you changed your mind about the whole advisor situation.

Then your sister dies and we either let this chick out of the bathroom or we don't.

> *Beat.*

MAXIMA. Okay.

> *They tie her up, gag her, and stick her in the bathroom. Talib Furozh blocks the door from inside the bathroom. The princess lies passed out, slumped against the toilet.*

Espanta!

Scene 4

> *Espanta pops her head in the door.*

MAXIMA. I've had a change of heart.

I wanna be Juana's puppet master.

ESPANTA. I know, I heard. I just told the Queen.

She's on her way back.

MAXIMA. Thanks Espanta.

ESPANTA. No worries.

> *Espanta exits. There is the extensive fanfare and light like from before when the Queen entered. But this time, Espanta and the Maid wheel her into the room in a royal-looking, tricked out wheelchair. They get her in clumsily and then bow out. HRH Queen Isabella intermittently takes hits off an oxygen mask.*

End of Act Three

ACT FOUR

Scene 1

HRH QUEEN ISABELLA. Our dear adopted sister,
How deeply overjoyed we are
To have news of your acceptance
Of God's decree
That you become advisor to our daughter,
The future Queen of Spain!
MAXIMA. Sure. It's not a problem! I'm all over it.
HRH QUEEN ISABELLA. How much peace it has given us in
our final hours to know our child
Will have your firm hand on the tiller of her ship.
MAXIMA. I'm about to steer that little sailboat straight to the is-
land of awesome.
HRH QUEEN ISABELLA. There is one small thing Maxima,
ahem, upon which we absolutely must insist.
MAXIMA. What's that?
HRH QUEEN ISABELLA. You have to believe in God.
Spain is a Christian nation; her people are a Christian people.
We must have proof that you are suited to lead a Christian country.
MAXIMA. Our Father, who art a shepherd,
Please lead Your flock of seagulls
Bursting into the sunshine of Jesus Christ Superstar,
Lord of the flies,
Full of grace-ful dancing and singing joyous Hallelujah.
On the mountaintop.
Amen.
HRH QUEEN ISABELLA. We did not find that to be a convincing
show of Christian zeal.
Look into my eyes Maxima.
This is what the voice of God sounds like to me:
Like the movement of a sandstorm,
Like the echo of the deepest ocean, like my soul's parent.
God's talking Maxima,

Though you may not understand Him He's talking.

MAXIMA. He's totally talking.

HRH QUEEN ISABELLA. But you're not listening.
We will not leave Spain in the hands of one
Who will not submit to fulfilling God's will on earth.

MAXIMA. Bullshit Isabella.
What? Was it God's will for you to oversee the deaths of millions of innocent people?
I know all about the shit that's going on in Hispaniola.
So don't try and tell me you were doing God's will when you plundered and decimated an entire civilization.

HRH QUEEN ISABELLA. What a very important facet of Christian leadership
You have brought up adopted sister.
The willingness to defend one's God and country
Even when bloodshed is required.
While we are personally saddened by the deaths of those lost souls unwilling to accept God's word, our God is a jealous God.
And the Catholic Church is the one true path.
Which means that anyone who believes other stuff,
Is an heretic that deserves only our wrath.
We are God's ever-willing handmaiden; We're just following orders.

MAXIMA. Then how about you follow the one that says that I get to be Juana's advisor and then leave me the heck alone?

HRH QUEEN ISABELLA. When God commanded Abraham to go to the mountaintop and kill Isaac,
Abraham's only son,
Abraham said "Yes Lord."
When God ordained us Queen, we took a vow to be a soldier of the Lord,
To protect Spain and the Holy Catholic Church.
And we have.

> *HRH Queen Isabella raps on the side of her royal wheelchair.*
> *The door to Maxima's bedchamber is opened and Abdul Haseeb*
> *is thrown roughly into the room with his hands bound and a*
> *hood over his head.*

An heretic, and enemy of Spain
Has been apprehended here on your very grounds.
Answer God's call just as Abraham did.
Take up the sword of devotion and defend Spain.

We will have proof of your faith before the sun sets today.

MAXIMA. Wait, you want me to kill him?

That's what you mean right?

You want me to murder an old man?

HRH QUEEN ISABELLA. Right now is the end of this conversation.

> *HRH Queen Isabella wheels her wheelchair unsteadily out of the room.*

Scene 2

ABDUL HASEEB. My lady Maxima, is that you?

> *From inside the bathroom:*

TALIB FUROZH. Abdul Haseeb?

MAXIMA. Well FUCK ME.

ABDUL HASEEB. It is you.

MAXIMA. We gotta figure out some way to get you out of here old man.

ESPANT—

ABDUL HASEEB. One moment, if you will, my lady Maxima.

If I'm to understand this correctly,

The Queen desires my life

As proof that you are fit to lead Spain?

MAXIMA. Yeah I'm pretty sure that's what just happened.

ABDUL HASEEB. And if you lead Spain, it might save the life of Talib Furozh

And many many others…

I'm an old man milady.

Surely all the lives that would be saved

Are worth the life of one exhausted old man.

TALIB FUROZH. No way Abdul Haseeb.

Don't do it Maxima.

ABDUL HASEEB. One man's life to save millions of lives.

There is a greater good milady.

TALIB FUROZH. No fucking way Maxima.

MAXIMA. Goddammit!

Just everybody shut up for one second okay!!!

It's like, here's a rock, here is me, and over there is a hard location.
THINK, mind!

A knock on the door.

Scene 3

MAXIMA. Who the fuck is it?!?
MAID. Room service.

*Maxima Terriblé Segunda shoves Abdul Haseeb into the armoire.
The Maid enters timidly and begins changing the linens on the
bed. She is so meek and unassuming that Maxima does not
have the heart to scream at her to leave. Maxima tosses herself
down on the divan, pooped but thinking fast. The Maid starts
humming then singing to herself the hymn...*

The Lord is my shepherd
I'll walk with Him always.
He knows me and He loves me
I'll walk with Him always.
Always. Always.
I'll walk with Him always.
He leads me by still waters,
I'll walk with Him always.
MAXIMA. What is your name?
MAID. Me?
MAXIMA. Who else would I be talking to right now?
MAID. Your pardon My Ladyship...
My name is Innocenzia.
MAXIMA. Innocenzia.
What was up with that song Innocenzia?
MAID. I'm sorry madam sometimes I sing things in my head and
I don't realize they're coming out of my mouth.
I've known it ever since I was a child.
Must have been from the sisters who raised me up Your Ladyship...
MAXIMA. Haven't you any parents Innocenzia?
MAID. I suppose we've all got parents Your Ladyship.
Only mine couldn't afford to bring me up and feed me and so

they put me in a bulrush basket outside of a convent right after I was born.

MAXIMA. Oh, right.

MAID. The sisters there found me and took me in and raised me up. Fed me and cared for me taught me proper so I could get a good job and all...

MAXIMA. A good job?

MAID. I'm awfully lucky Your Ladyship.
Luckier than most—got clothes, food, a warm place to sleep nights.
I even got a whole real for Christ's Mass last year!

MAXIMA. One real?

MAID. I gave it right to the sisters Your Ladyship,
"He who is kind to the poor lends to the LORD, and the Lord will reward him for what he has done."
That's what the Bible says.
And the sisters got so many other children to take care of just like me.

MAXIMA. You believe in God, Innocenzia?

MAID. I love God, Your Ladyship.
Who else but God would have watched over that little baby in that bulrush basket outside the convent gates?
Seen that I didn't get eaten up by a wild animal or fall into cruel hands?
I'm just about the luckiest person I know, Your Ladyship.
How could I not believe in God?

MAXIMA. Innocenzia,
Sorry if I'm getting too personal here,
But you seem pretty Christian and all so
Would you be willing to kill someone for God?

MAID. How could that be, Your Ladyship?
God said it right in the Bible
Commandment number six
"Thou shalt not kill."
So, I don't really understand how it could come to that
But I suppose I'm simple and might not really know...

MAXIMA. Yeah maybe not.

Innocenzia stares at the map.

MAID. Forgive me if I'm being impertinent Your Ladyship,
But I've never seen drawings like these before...

MAXIMA. They're maps.
They're drawings of what the world looks like.

If you were looking down on the Earth from the sky, That's what you would see.

MAID. So then that must be what the world looks like to God? Your Ladyship has drawn a picture of the world just as God sees it!

MAXIMA. Yeah I guess so.

MAID. It all just looks so small from this angle.
The people who live in the places on this map
Must be even so much smaller. Like children.
I suppose that's why God treats all of us like his children.
With patience and love.
But I suppose I don't know much about maps after all Your Ladyship.
I'm just *a simple hunchback bastard child that someone found in a bulrush basket.*

> *A golden light glows from behind her as she speaks that line.*

Will you require anything else right now your ladyship?

MAXIMA. No Innocenzia, that will be all for now.

> *The Maid stumbles upon the crumpled up wanted flyer on the floor. She picks it up, looks at it and sticks it in her pocket and leaves.*

Scene 4

> *Maxima hobbles over to the armoire and releases Abdul Haseeb.*

MAXIMA. C'mere old-timer.

> *In the bathroom, Infanta Juana wakes up and starts kicking and trying to scream. Talib Furozh very calmly pulls out a 9mm and aims it at her. He cocks the gun. The gun should totally be anachronistic in this world.*

TALIB FUROZH. Shut your freaking mouth or I will shoot you right now.

> *Infanta Juana shuts up.*

ABDUL HASEEB. You will find a small dagger tucked under the right side of my belt, milady.

Back in the bathroom:

TALIB FUROZH. I was there, under the covers before.
I heard what you said about the New World…
And you ignorant dicks have no fucking idea what you're talking
about.
I watch you people on Fox News running your mouths,
Spinning absolutely anything horrible that you feel like doing
Into a dictate from God
Or a way to preserve the country.
And peaceful people everywhere just keep bending over
And letting people like you take whatever the hell it is that you want.

    Infanta Juana starts to say something.

Shut up.

    Bedroom:

    *Maxima Terriblé Segunda pulls out the dagger. She holds it
    really awkwardly.*

MAXIMA. Abdul Haseeb, I can't…
ABDUL HASEEB. I've made my peace Lady Maxima.
This won't take you but a moment…
TALIB FUROZH. Scream or attract attention to yourself in any way
And you will die before anyone hears you.
ABDUL HASEEB. I have dedicated my life to service, Lady Maxima.
And now, with one small flick of that dagger,
My life will serve innocent people the world over.
Pull my head up and back Lady Maxima, and I will feel little pain.

    Talib Furozh removes Infanta Juana's gag.

INFANTA JUANA. I said,
You're just like me.
You and I are just exactly the same.
TALIB FUROZH. I honestly cannot wait until people like you are
naturally selected out of existing…
INFANTA JUANA. We both know what we want
And we're both willing to kill in order to get what we want.
Right?
So you're about to kill me
For saying I'd be willing to do the exact same thing
That you're contemplating doing to me right now?
TALIB FUROZH. Maxima said you were crazy…

INFANTA JUANA. Well, is it more or less crazy to hit someone
on the head
And then lock them in the bathroom?
You're not a better person than I am.
The only real difference between you and me
Is that I was accidentally born rich and powerful
And you were accidentally born poor and persecuted.

> *Bedroom.*

MAXIMA. Abdul Haseeb, I'm sorry. I'm so sorry.

> *Abdul Haseeb begins to sing a prayer in Arabic. Bathroom—*

INFANTA JUANA. Right?
Killing me won't change anything.
It'll just make you more like exactly what you hate.

> *Talib Furozh lowers the gun. He slaps the gag back on her
> mouth with some force. In the bedroom—*

MAXIMA. I'm sorry.
I can't do it.

> *Maxima Terriblé Segunda removes his hood, cuts his hands
> free. She pushes Abdul Haseeb out the trapdoor.*

Go on now. GIT!
Espanta!!

Scene 5

> *Espanta bursts right in.*

ESPANTA. Did you do it?!?
MAXIMA. No.
ESPANTA. I knew it.
This is a problem.
Remember before when the Queen said that you had to kill him
before the sun set?
MAXIMA. I know.

To Audience:

ESPANTA. Ah!
The great secret of my heart-breast!
The prophecy about the cold!
I feel them… starting… to converge—
Oh no, the Queen!

Espanta scampers away. Talib pops out of the bathroom.

TALIB FUROZH. Did you do it?
MAXIMA. No. She still breathing?
TALIB FUROZH. Yeah.
MAXIMA. Talib my love, you have to go.
If they find you, they'll kill you.
Take this gold, grab our maps and go.
TALIB FUROZH. Maxima baby, there's nowhere on this map I want to go that doesn't have you.

Scene 6

Fanfare. HRH Queen Isabella is rolled onto the stage on her actual deathbed.

HRH QUEEN ISABELLA. Maxima?

Infanta Juana squeals from the bathroom. Talib Furozh aims the gun at her again.

What was that sound?
MAXIMA. Nothing. The cats.
HRH QUEEN ISABELLA. So… have you committed your act of faith?
MAXIMA. No. I let him go.
HRH QUEEN ISABELLA. You let a terrorist who conspired to Burn down a government building go free?
We have had it with you Maxima.
You have failed us.
GUARDS!!
MAXIMA. Wait just one second Isabella.

You remember when God told you that thing
About making a lowly hunchback advisor to the Queen?
I think it's possible that he had someone else in mind.
Innocenzia!!
HRH QUEEN ISABELLA. This had better be good Maxima…
MAXIMA. Don't worry, it will be.

Scene 7

The Maid rushes in.

MAID. Your Ladyship?
MAXIMA. This is her Isabella.
This is the girl who should actually be Juana's advisor.
She is gentle and good,
Raised by nuns.
Patient and without judgment.
There is Juana's advisor, not me.
HRH QUEEN ISABELLA. Are you a lowly hunchback bastard
that was found in a bulrush basket?
MAID. I am.
HRH QUEEN ISABELLA. Do you believe in God?
MAID. I love God, Your Highness.
HRH QUEEN ISABELLA. And my child,
One further question.
Would you be willing to take up the sword of justice
To defend the name of the Lord and His church?

The golden light starts shining from the Maid as she speaks.

MAID. Forgive me Your Majesty but,
"If I speak in the tongues of men or of angels, but do not have
love, I am only a resounding gong or a clanging cymbal. If I have
the gift of prophecy and can fathom all mysteries and all knowledge, and if I have a faith that can move mountains, but do not
have love, I am nothing. If I give all I possess to the poor and give
over my body to hardship that I may boast, but do not have love,
I gain nothing."

Your Majesty, were I advisor to the Queen, I admit that I would let lie the sword of justice for the Lord Himself to wield.
I, Your Majesty, would take up the banner of love...
HRH QUEEN ISABELLA. So basically, no.
Just so we're clear,
Your answer to my question I asked you before about killing people for God is no.
And you still let a terrorist run free.
GUARDS!!!

End of Act Four

ACT FIVE

Scene 1

A knock on the door. A man in an official-looking uniform enters.

DEPUTY GOVERNOR OF HISPANIOLA. Your pardon, Your Royal Highness.
But I was told that the child in question was to be found in this bedchamber.
HRH QUEEN ISABELLA. Reveal to us your name and title sir.
DEPUTY GOVERNOR OF HISPANIOLA. My name is Eduardo D'Ávila y León, Your Royal Highness.
I am the Deputy Governor of Hispaniola.
I've a warrant for the arrest of the Moor Talib Furozh,
Math tutor and enemy of the Spanish Crown.
> *The Maid breaks rank.*

MAID. You've come!
It was I who sent for you milord.
I found the man you were looking for,
The one from the picture.
I saw that very same rakish hat and cloak this morning.
> *She pulls out the wanted poster.*

He's in the bathroom.
When might I claim my reward?
DEPUTY GOVERNOR OF HISPANIOLA. The Moor in question is in this lady's washroom?
MAID. YES!
Can I have my money please.
HRH QUEEN ISABELLA. I banished that very man to the colonies myself three years ago today...
MAXIMA. Innocenzia!
How could you betray me in this fashion?

MAID. But how have I betrayed you, Your Ladyship?
1,000 reales milady to give to the nuns.
For the capture of a bad man,
That's what the poster says, right?
I can't really read.

>*The Deputy Governor of Hispaniola bangs on the bathroom door.*

DEPUTY GOVERNOR OF HISPANIOLA. Talib Furozh!!
Open this door right now, for you are under arrest!
ESPANTA. WAIT JUST ONE SECOND.
Everybody just chill the fuck out for one second okay?
The great secret of my heart-breast,
The prophecy of the cold,
AGGGHHHH!!!!
I can no longer contain it.
It must be revealed!

Scene 2

>*Espanta darts out of the room. Everyone waits. It takes kind*
>*of a long time. Finally she comes back. She pulls out a gross-*
>*looking little piece of rope out of her gigantic bosom.*

ESPANTA. THIS is proof.
Of a great secret that I have carried for so very long in my heart-breast.
HRH QUEEN ISABELLA. What is that gross-looking little piece
of rope?
ESPANTA. Forgive me Your Royal Highness but it is your umbilical
cord.

>*She turns to Maxima Terriblé Segunda.*

And also your umbilical cord.
MAXIMA. How can this be?
ESPANTA. Come here you, and you.
Maxima the story of finding you in a bulrush basket is a false lie.
Once upon a time, fifty-two years ago,
A royal lady gave birth to a pair of twin baby girls.

The first baby born was christened Isabella and welcomed with open arms.
But to prevent the wagging of stuck up tongues,
The second twin, a hunchback,
Was placed outside the palace gates in a bulrush basket…

> *Espanta pulls them aside and walks them through how the ends of the dried-up little umbilical cord exactly fits both of their belly buttons. They "Ooh" and "Ahh" and "It's the very same shape as my belly button! It must be true."*

MAXIMA. My twin sister…
HRH QUEEN ISABELLA. *My* twin sister…
MAXIMA. Whoa. You were right Espanta, that was a big secret.
ESPANTA. Right?
DEPUTY GOVERNOR OF HISPANIOLA. Pardon me Your Highness but I feel I must interject.
For you see,
In addition to being the Deputy Governor of Hispaniola,
I am also a widely acknowledged expert on the laws of succession
Within the Spanish monarchy.
HRH QUEEN ISABELLA. Oh really?
Show us your badge of expertise.

> *He shows her.*

We are satisfied.
DEPUTY GOVERNOR OF HISPANIOLA. Your Royal Highness,
As I'm sure any other leading expert in my field could tell you,
It is a clear-cut and firmly established rule in Spain
That the throne passes from first-born twin to second-born twin.
So basically…
HRH QUEEN ISABELLA. When I pass, sister…
MAXIMA. Don't say such a thing sister.
HRH QUEEN ISABELLA. Shhhhh…
When I pass, you will be Queen.
And in light of all this new information,
Methinks this bastard hunchback child would actually be a really good advisor to the Queen.
MAID. Thanks, Your Majesty.
MAXIMA. Whoa. I can't believe how good everything just worked out.
EVERYONE. Hooray!!

HRH QUEEN ISABELLA. All hail the next Queen of Spain, Her Royal Highness Maxima Terriblé Segunda!!

> *They all bow low. Infanta Juana hears all of this from inside the bathroom. In a flash, she rises and blows out the candles. The bathroom goes dark. A moment later we hear two gunshots. Talib Furozh emerges from the bathroom, clutching a bleeding wound on his chest.*

TALIB FUROZH. Maxima!!

MAXIMA. Talib my love!!

> *Infanta Juana emerges, splattered in blood. She guns down the Maid.*

INFANTA JUANA. And fuck you too, Auntie M.

> *Infanta Juana shoots Maxima Terriblé Segunda. Maxima, Talib, and the Maid all die.*

Anyone else?
Didn't think so.

The End

Epilogue

After people speak their lines, they leave the stage.

ESPANTA. If we Spaniards have offended,
Think but this and all is mended.
INFANTA JUANA. The tragic ending of our play,
Might have gone down a different way.
HRH QUEEN ISABELLA. Spain's momentary rise to power
Was a millisecond in eternity's hour.
ABDUL HASEEB. That pow'rful bloodthirsty regime
Was just as fleeting as a dream.
TALIB FUROZH. So let it be a lesson to us all:
As empires rise, so do they fall.
MAID. Is there a God? Well who can say.
But one thing that we've learned today:

> *Only the blood-splattered Hunchback of Seville remains onstage in her own light.*

MAXIMA. I once heard Tony Kushner speak in Minneapolis and he said that
Artists have a responsibility to err on the side of hope,
And I agree with that…
So walk away with what you will,
From the tale of the Hunchback of Seville.

End of Play

PROPERTY LIST

Spanish flag
Drum and fife
Weapons
The Compendious Book on Calculation by Completion and Balancing
Feather duster
Coconut on velvet pillow
Letter
"Wanted" flyer
Doll
Maps
Cane
Turkey leg
Cell phone
Rope and gag
Oxygen mask
Wheelchair
Gun
Dagger
Umbilical cord
Badge

SOUND EFFECTS

Water splashing
Musket fire, screams, ocean waves, and Arabic music
Extensive fanfare
Gunshots

9780822235552